THE
PERFECT
BOARD

CALVIN K. CLEMONS, CAE, CMP

OVATION
Books

SECOND EDITION

The Perfect Board
Published by Ovation Books
PO Box 80107
Austin, Texas 78758

For more information about our books, please write to us, email us at info@ovationbooks.com, or visit our website at www.ovationbooks.net.

Distributed to the trade by National Book Network, Inc.

ISBN-13: 978-0-9790275-6-7
ISBN: 0-9790275-6-X

Copyright© 2008 by Calvin K. Clemons
Third printing, 2009
Library of Congress Cataloging-in-Publication Data

Clemons, Calvin K.
  The perfect board / by Calvin K. Clemons.-- 2nd ed.
    p. cm.
  Includes bibliographical references.
  ISBN-13: 978-0-9790275-6-7 (hardcover : alk. paper)
  ISBN-10: 0-9790275-6-X (hardcover : alk. paper)
  1. Boards of directors. 2. Directors of corporations. 3. Corporate governance. 4. Management. I. Title.
  HD2745.C497 2007
  658.4'22--dc22
                                        2007024565

10 9 8 7 6 5 4 3 2

CONTENTS

Acknowledgements v

Foreword vii

Introduction ix

Rebecca's Awakening 1

The Visit 6

Seeing the Book 10

Beginning 14

Loyalty 17

Obedience 19

Care 20

Obligation 22

Confidentiality 23

Competency 25

Do It Right 27

Respect 29

Unity 31

Willingness 32

Open Minded 33

Leadership 34

Delegation 35

Conflicts of Interest 37

Diversity 39

Care of the Organization's Property 41

Honesty 42

Meetings 44

Meeting Attendance 46

Quorum 48
Rules of Order 50
The Ayes Have It! 52
Voting 53
Ballot 55
Minutes 57
Bylaws 59
Public Scrutiny 62
Tax-Exempt Organizations 64
Compensation 67
Excess Compensation 69
Reimbursement 71
Indemnification 73
Directors and Officers Insurance 75
Antitrust Considerations 76
Volunteer Protection 78
Sarbanes-Oxley Act 80
Audit Committee 82
Forbidden Fruit 83
Lawyers 85
Executive Sessions 87
Executive Committees 89
The Abilene Paradox 91
Orientation 93
Strategic Planning 95
Ending 97
Dinner With E.J 99
Epilogue 105
Bibliography 109

Acknowledgements

Through the years, there are many people who have helped me, and I thank them all.

Some who deserve special mention include Bob Harris, Mary Jane Kolar, Jeff Glassie, Cathy Larrabee, Crista LeGrand, Robert Liberto, Rick Wolfe, Curt and Liz Matterson, Tom and Liz Pawlak, Anne Leimbach, Peter and Sue Berry, Michael Sherman, Greg Melia, Tim Holt, John Buckley, Hugh Mallon, Don Frendburg, Ed McMillan and Jill Cornish.

Special thanks to my wife, Theresa, who has been a support to me more than she can ever know.

FOREWORD

With more than a million non-profit organizations in the United States, volunteers have the opportunity to express their leadership skills by serving on boards of directors. From trade associations and professional societies to the PTA, church board, chamber of commerce or city council, this book is a collection of the most important aspects of Board service.

The Perfect Board has proven to be the quick-read primer for volunteer leaders. Whether you give the book to the officers at the installation ceremony, or provide copies to the entire Board, every page offers practical tips.

By distributing the book in advance of the annual leadership orientation meeting, Directors have time to read and come prepared with questions. For example, reading the chapter on "conflicts of interest" opens a discussion on what might qualify as a conflict and how to avoid them.

The Perfect Board is comprehensive. Without it, many topics could be overlooked at the leadership orientation. While each chapter demonstrates the extensive experience of author Cal Clemons, he also covers the current affairs facing Boards. This includes the influence of the Sarbanes Oxley Act on non-profits, the $10 million dollar impact of antitrust violations, and important distinctions in Board and staff roles.

The Perfect Board is recommended for staff as well. The book reveals key aspects for staff to consider when interacting with the Board and committees.

Finally, while the adjective "perfect" may seem a lofty description, this book sets the tone for a committed leader to enrich the organization and strive for greatness during the Board experience.

Robert C. Harris, CAE

INTRODUCTION

There is a need for a simplified, down-to-earth guide for being a member of a Board of Directors. There are countless books, pamphlets and videotapes dedicated to this subject. Many are informative and educational. Some are tiring and unappealing, even though they are accurate. Some are also complicated and foreboding; others just don't make the grade.

The purpose of this book is to create a primer that is easy to understand, allowing people to realize that being on a Board of Directors is a wonderful experience. Moreover, it is usually an honor, and definitely recognition, from one's contemporaries and associates. However, it comes with responsibilities and duties.

In today's world of increased accountability and heightened legislative activity, it is more important than ever to understand that a Director must be fully aware of what goes on behind the doors of the Boardroom. No longer can an individual just sit back and accept the accolades and benefits of being on the Board. That Director is now under increased scrutiny. He or she has to appreciate the weight of doing the right thing and the responsibility and accountability that come with the position.

With over a quarter century of working with Boards of Directors, I have seen and heard many things. I have witnessed great leaders who have put their Director positions ahead of their own personal position with the company or organization. I have seen people grow and become outstanding Directors. I have experienced success after being involved in hard-won battles and carefully crafted plans and programs.

But I have seen the other side as well: inconsistency where there should have been consistency and dishonesty where there should have been integrity. I have seen people do egregious acts to others in order to make themselves look better.

Perhaps some people will use this primer, take it seriously . . . and become members of "The Perfect Board."

Rebecca's Awakening

Rebecca just discovered she had been nominated to the Board of Directors. She was thrilled by the recognition of her peers. She had been selected from a large group of qualified people, some of whom she thought were more capable and more experienced than she was.

She was excited about the things she would be able to get done when she had been elected. Rebecca was not trying to be presumptuous in her thoughts, but everyone knew that when someone received the nomination, election to the Board was all but certain. In fact, the joke was "the train went right through the station!"

Then it hit her.

Oh my goodness, she thought, *I really don't know anything about being on a Board of Directors except for what I have heard and seen this Board do. I've done some reading, but I really don't know what I should . . . or for that matter . . . shouldn't do.*

Her thoughts began to swirl.

Don't get rattled, she thought.

Rebecca's college degree was in marketing; she was a good thinker. She had worked her way up to vice president of marketing of a major company. She knew what was important and how to value time. But in all of her training and educational development, there was nothing about serving on a Board of Directors. She had not studied the subject, nor did she know much about it.

"Marcus, I need your help," she barked into the telephone.

"Becca, you always need my help!" replied the male voice on the other end.

"Seriously, I really need your help!"

"Seriously, Becca, what can be so serious?" asked Marcus.

"Stop being silly, Marcus. I do need your help. Perhaps you can give me a bit of guidance about this new position."

"You get promoted?"

Rebecca replied, "No, Marcus. I did not get promoted. I've been nominated to the Board of Directors of the Association."

"That's great, Becca. Congratulations!!"

There was a brief pause.

"But Becca, we should be drinking champagne or wine instead of you looking for help. Don't you think?"

Quickly, Rebecca replied, "Marcus, I need your help because I really don't know the first thing about being on a Board of Directors. There are quite a few people on this Board who will be observing me closely, and I don't want to screw up or do anything wrong. That's why I am asking you for help."

With a comforting voice, Marcus provided help.

"Becca, meet me tomorrow night at the Trinity Lounge. We'll have a glass of wine to celebrate the occasion. Then, we'll talk about what you can do to prepare yourself for this new opportunity."

"I knew I could count on you Marcus. Tomorrow at six?"

"See you then."

The wind was light but chilly as Rebecca entered the Trinity Lounge. Marcus was already there waiting. Two glasses of red wine rested on the table set apart by one of those candles flamed by some sort of fluid.

"Merlot?" asked Rebecca.

"The only kind I drink," Marcus said as he arose to greet the tall woman dressed in a handsome blue tweed suit. His hands lightly grabbed her arms and he gracefully kissed her cheek.

"It's good to see you, Becca," as he motioned to her to sit down.

"Marcus, it is always good to see you."

She raised her glass to his, and the two toasted each other.

He propped both elbows on the table, looked her in the eye and said, "Okay, now what's up?"

"Oh, you're always to the point. That's what I like about you." She took a sip of the red wine. "I told you last night that I was nominated for the Board of Directors."

"Yes, I know."

"Let me finish. I have a college degree and am vice president of marketing for a major company, but I don't know the first thing about being on a Board of Directors. It worries me because I am the type of person who likes to know what I am supposed to do."

"It's not hard."

"I never said anything about it being hard. I said I want to know what I am supposed to do. You know, responsibilities, duties, tasks and whatever else."

"There are books."

"C'mon, Marcus. Books! Books can't have all the answers. Besides, I've already checked the library and there's not much there. I also checked on the Internet. No treasures there either. There just has to be something else, some other way to find out."

"Well, there is this gentleman who has worked in the field for a lot of years. I heard only today from another friend that he is sort of the leading authority on Boards of Directors and organizational governance."

"Tell me who it is!"

"Easy, Becca, one step at a time."

"What do you mean? I have a situation and you have an answer, and you say 'one step at a time.' C'mon, Marcus, share your information."

He leaned back in the chair and a wry smile cracked his face.

"Becca, I don't know this man or much about him,

but my friend says that this fellow has invented what he calls 'The Perfect Board.'"

"The Perfect Board?"

"Yes, 'The Perfect Board.'"

"Tell me more."

The Visit

It was about a four-hour drive to the house. As Becca entered the oval driveway, she guessed the house to be over one hundred years old. The white columns on the front porch reflected antebellum architecture; the magnolia trees and rose bushes only reinforced her feelings.

"Is Mr. Edward Cummings at home?" she asked the woman who opened the front door of the beautiful house.

"Hello, I assume you are Rebecca Mayfield. You will find Mr. Cummings on the back porch. He is expecting you."

Becca looked at the woman and felt welcomed.

"Oh, I am so sorry. My name is Olivia. I help Mr. Cummings from time to time, especially when he has visitors such as yourself."

"That's okay, I understand. Can I just walk around back? The grounds are so nice."

Olivia answered quickly. "Yes, of course. In fact, he

6

prefers that guests walk through the rose garden. He's ever so proud of it. You can head right through that path." She pointed to her right and motioned Becca to walk to the left side of the house.

"Thank you, Olivia."

Becca walked around to the side of the house and discovered a well-manicured and maintained rose garden. There were dozens of varieties and many colors. The fragrance was inspiring. She could hear the bees busily working at their pollinating tasks, and the sound of flight broke the warm afternoon silence.

As she rounded the back of the house, there was another stately, impressive porch with columns. It faced the river that lay about a hundred yards down a terraced slope of green grass. Everywhere there were oak and maple trees with a sweet gum or hickory tree thrown in for variety. The setting was magnificent.

There were four white rocking chairs on the porch. They all faced the river. One was occupied by an elderly gentleman. She walked up the steps of the porch and smiled.

"Hello, I am Rebecca Mayfield. We talked on the telephone."

The man rose to his feet and offered his hand.

"Yes, I know, Miss Mayfield. I am pleased to meet you. I am Edward Cummings, but I prefer to be called E.J."

"E.J. is a very nice name," answered Becca. "Is it a family name?"

"Oh, no, not at all. When I was in college, my fraternity brothers shortened Edward John to E.J. and it has stuck ever since. Please sit down." He motioned her to one of the rocking chairs.

"Mr. Cummings, oh, I'm sorry, E.J., this is a beautiful setting. I cannot believe how peaceful and quiet it is."

"Miss Mayfield," he started.

Becca interrupted. "If I call you E.J., then I insist you call me Becca. It's short for Rebecca and I like my friends to use it."

"All right, Becca," he smiled at her. "I like that name, Becca. It has charm."

He continued. "Becca, I bought this place many years ago. I needed somewhere to go to escape the fast pace and complexities of the world. It had grown too hectic. My wife and I came here almost twenty years ago. She really loved this house. And, she loved her roses, too."

Becca remarked, "The roses are lovely. But you said 'she loved her roses,' correct?"

"Yes, unfortunately she passed away several years ago. I loved her very much. She meant the world to me. Keeping the rose garden tended is my tribute to her."

"You are to be commended."

"How so?" he asked.

"Well, for paying tribute, as you say, to her. People just don't do enough of those kinds of things. We all think we're too busy and there's not enough time. And, you should be congratulated for the roses, too. I have never seen such a beautiful garden."

He laughed. "Don't give me any credit for the roses. I just look at them like you do. Ernesto gets all the credit.

He is Olivia's brother. In fact, he deserves the credit for all of the yard work. He does a splendid job, don't you think?"

"He certainly deserves a lot of credit. This must be quite a job."

"It is, but you are not here to discuss my landscaping and gardens, are you?"

"You're right, E.J. My purpose in coming is about a different treasure. I believe that treasure lies within you, and I am told that you have a wealth of knowledge about Boards of Directors."

"Lemonade?" He poured a glass for her, and then one for himself.

"Becca, I have spent my life working for, in, through and around Boards. They come in all sizes and shapes. I firmly believe that Boards are the backbone of democracy. We learn how to share ideas, reach decisions and take action through Boards."

E.J. continued.

"I think there is a lot to learn about Boards, and I am glad you came. I believe I can teach you a lot. However, it will take time. Are you ready?"

Becca had stopped rocking and leaned forward on the front of the chair.

"Oh, yes, I am prepared."

"Good, let's start."

He stood and motioned for her to stand.

"Let's go to the library. My notes are there."

SEEING THE BOOK

Rebecca and E.J. went into the library. There was a large oak desk sitting just to the left of the stone fireplace. Books filled the shelves of the built-in bookcases. Leather chairs and side tables were strategically placed throughout the room. She felt a warmness and a sense of welcome as she entered the room.

"Please sit down, and we'll begin," E.J. said as he motioned for her to sit in the red leather chair immediately adjacent to the desk.

"Thank you," she replied and eased herself into the cool leather.

E.J. shuffled some papers on his desk, and then opened the left hand drawer. He pulled out a green leather book that looked similar to a ledger. He put it down on the desk in front of him. He brushed the top as if there were dust, but there was none.

Looking directly at Becca, E.J. said, "I have worked in the business of organizations all my life. I have seen many people come and go. I have seen many organizations succeed and more fail. Oh, maybe I should not say fail, because they did continue on. What I should say is I have seen many organizations fail . . . fail to accomplish or achieve what they could have."

"Why is that?"

"Becca, it's people that can make a difference. Whether it's a Board, company or association or even a church group, people truly can change the outcome from success to failure."

E.J. sat back in the swivel chair and rubbed his chin with his left hand.

"You see, Becca, I don't think that anyone starts out to harm an organization. Oh, yes, there are some bad apples, and I guess there always will be. I am not talking about those because they only make up a small percentage of Board members. Most people have very good intentions, like you."

Becca relaxed a bit and sat back in her chair. She said, "Yes, and that's why I am here. I do have good intentions, and I really take my new position seriously."

"I know you do or you would not have driven all this distance to visit with me."

"That's correct!"

E.J. grinned and continued.

"Organizations fail to realize their potential because the individuals elected or appointed to lead them just plain don't know how! It really is that simple."

"No one goes to school for this. There are no real educational courses for Board service. Of course there are

11

books, and now Web sites, available that provide some information. But, all in all, the information deals more with the mechanics than with actual experience. That's where I come in."

He patted the green leather booklet.

"In this file, I have assembled what I call 'The Perfect Board.' It is my life's work. I have identified the precepts of what I believe it takes to truly have an organization, big or small, succeed, get things done and avoid all that fighting and rancor that seems to come with the territory. I've kept this material to myself, except of course when I was counseling Boards. But I am getting older, and I now realize that I can no longer consult or advise every organization on these precepts. So, I am ready to share it with the world. And that's why I allowed you to visit me today."

"Really?" Becca asked as she slid forward to the front of her chair.

"Yes, really." E.J. leaned forward and flipped open the cover of the book. "It all starts here. Would you like to read it?"

"Are you kidding me? Of course I want to read it."

"Good. Very good."

He closed the cover and handed the book to her.

She felt the weight of the book as he passed it to her. It was heavier than she'd thought. She grasped it with both hands and placed it on her lap. She softly rubbed the green leather.

E.J. stood and, with a stern expression, said, "Becca, you have to read it here. I cannot allow the book to leave this house . . . at least not at this time."

"I understand."

"You see, I was not sure I was going to share this with you. I was impressed by your telephone call, but I needed to meet you to determine whether or not you would be the person for the job."

"Job?"

"Yes, for sure, a job. Mind you, it's not a regular job though. It's more of a challenge than a job. *Harrumph.* That's enough of that. I'll tell you more later. For the present, I'll leave you here to read."

"Make yourself comfortable. Curl up on the sofa if you wish. If you need anything, just ask Olivia. She'll gladly assist you."

Becca's eyes grew large with astonishment and she watched him as he walked toward the door.

E.J. looked back at her. "I know this is not what you expected, but please believe me, it will make a difference for you. Now, I'll take my leave and you can read. I'll be back in," he looked at his watch, "let's say an hour and a half. That should do it."

"But I don't underst . . . ."

He interrupted her before she could finish, "Becca, just trust me on this. I'll see you later."

The door closed. It was quiet. She sat back in the chair and brought her right leg up under her left leg so that her right ankle was under her left knee. Awkward, but comfortable.

She opened the book . . . .

BEGINNING

We all aspire to perfection. It is a natural drive within us to make sure things work well and are as good as they can be.

"The Perfect Board" is a set of precepts and ideas that can enable people, even the uninitiated, to work together . . . effectively . . . efficiently . . . and harmoniously to achieve the goals of the organization.

This country was founded as an organization. Its goals were . . . and are . . . the pursuit of happiness, protection of property and basic human freedoms. The U.S. Constitution is the document that governs all of us. It establishes a system of governance that is divided into three parts: executive, judicial and legislative. Most Americans understand this concept.

The U.S. Constitution is the bedrock for all of our organizations, large or small, profit or non-profit, national or local, city or town, volunteer or paid.

This is an important distinction. Our democracy is based on this document. It is the fundamental premise that guarantees our freedoms. One of those freedoms is the right to come together and form organizations. That is something Americans have done since the beginning and continue to do. We are the models for how people join together in organizations for the overall good of our way of life. No other country can boast of such an endeavor.

The U.S. Constitution is the "law of the land." All other documents may complement it, but none can replace it. Understanding this foundation is essential because Directors must appreciate that organizations have governing documents that outline how the organization is structured and operates. Often, these documents include the Articles of Incorporation and Bylaws. In a way then, organizations have constitutions. In earlier times, these documents were even called the "Constitution and Bylaws." Some organizations still use these names when formulating their governing documents.

Now, on to the purpose of the Board. Just as the Constitution establishes representative government, so too do most organizations. It would be impractical to have every person participate in every activity of an organization. The members, stakeholders, stockholders or owners of the organization elect, select or appoint people to represent them in carrying out the mission of the organization.

This creates an orderly process for managing the organization, and it is called representative governance. Imagine the chaos of everyone gathered together trying to move the organization forward without any guideline to help them. It would be nearly impossible. It could be called "mob rule."

Understand this point clearly when discussing representative governance: representatives are entrusted to perform their duties and responsibilities as if they were the people they represent. They must adhere to a set of practices that ensures they measure up to this trust.

Having this knowledge firmly in mind, it is now time to explore "The Perfect Board."

LOYALTY

When taking office as a Director, whether appointed or elected, loyalty to the organization moves to the top rung of the ladder. The Director must put aside individual interests; this includes considerations for the Director's family, friends, associates, other organizations and above all, the Director's employer.

In some organizations, the illustration used is "the wearing of hats." Simply stated, a Director puts on the "hat" of the organization when elected or appointed to the Board. All other hats are removed and put aside. The Director then acts on behalf of the organization while wearing the "hat" of the organization.

As a Director, the organization's interests and well-being are considered instead of private or concealed interest.

The Director must commit allegiance to the organization and be unbiased in his or her decisions and actions.

Some organizations have commitment and allegiance forms that are signed by new Directors prior to taking office. In this way, the Director knows beforehand exactly what loyalty means both individually and as interpreted by the Board and the organization itself.

OBEDIENCE

Directors have the duty to be obedient to the organization. Inherent in the concept of obedience is following both the "letter" and the "spirit" of its governing documents. This includes the Articles of Incorporation, Bylaws, policies and any special orders.

In addition, Directors must ensure that the organization complies with any applicable federal, state and local laws.

CARE

As a Director, you are expected to use the care that an ordinary person would exercise in the same or similar position. This usually means that you must attend meetings, be informed, make reasonable decisions and see to it that things get done.

Attending meetings is essential. Failure to be present does not absolve a Director from responsibility. If you cannot attend Board meetings, then you must either decline a Board position or resign from it if you are already a Director.

A Director must be informed. It is not acceptable to say you did not know about an issue. It is your duty to be fully aware of the Board's issues and actions. Moreover, a Director must insure that the organization gathers the information necessary to explore the issues and make thoughtful decisions.

Thoughtful decisions follow a thorough, reasoned process. Directors have to read, review and study materials pertaining to each issue. They must be prepared to speak or provide input as well as actively participate in discussions and deliberations.

The decisions must be correctly recorded and filed. An appropriate document retention and disposal policy is vital to any organization's record keeping process.

Directors need to make sure things get done. It is not their responsibility to actually perform the activities or tasks, but they must make certain that, when delegated, the work is done or actions get accomplished. Courts will not accept the notion "someone else was supposed to do it."

Obligation

Make no mistake about it, the principle duty of the Board of Directors, and thereby of each Director, is to lead and care for the organization. This authority is passed along by law but obligations accompany it.

Directors are responsible for acting in the best interests of the organization. They are to use sound judgment, prudence and diligence in discharging their responsibilities. Wise Directors use the same benchmarks of performance for the organization as they would in running their own businesses.

Fiduciary responsibility is extremely important, and Directors sometimes practice spending the organization's money "as if it were their own." This is a good measure so long as the Director does not become so restrictive that the necessary funds are not provided to ensure the sound operation of the organization.

CONFIDENTIALITY

There is a saying, "What goes on at a Board of Directors' meeting, stays in the meeting!"

This simply means that information shared within the Board of Directors must be kept confidential. Discussions, votes and sensitive data must be protected. The right of Directors to speak out and voice their opinions without fear of recrimination is vital to the effective functioning of a Board.

Disgruntled Directors, or just those who disagree with an outcome, must understand that to carry the issue outside the Boardroom can cause great damage not only to the Board but also to the organization as well. By revealing confidential information, working relationships can be undermined and the effectiveness of the Board to get its job done can truly be compromised.

However, confidentiality concerns do not eliminate the Board's responsibility to regularly report its activities and decisions to the entire organization. Confidentiality is not a heavy cloak that allows the Board to tread in unlawful or illegal areas.

Some organizations use a confidentiality statement that is to be signed by each Director to remind them of the organization's position on confidentiality. The statement can also be made a part of the Director's commitment statement.

COMPETENCY

A Director needs to be competent.
The selection of competent persons begins with the leadership development or nominating committee learning about people's abilities, background, experience and skills before they become Directors. An organization has to have people working in positions and areas in which they can prove themselves to be both competent and capable of fulfilling the role of Director.

Participation in committees, task forces and other organizational activities often shows how well a person accomplishes assignments and gets along with others. This process can be viewed as the organization's "farm system."

Compared to major league baseball's farm system, people work their way "up" in the organization. As they perform successfully at each level and succeed, the person goes on to the next higher plateau of performance.

Seldom does a "rookie" break into the starting line-up of a major league baseball team. The same is true of a Board. Why let a rookie serve as a member on the Board when they have little knowledge about the Board or its issues?

Competency is learned. It is the combination of real life experience coupled with education. For some, competency comes earlier and more easily just as with some talented rookies. For others, it takes longer. Whatever the time element, the Director must be willing to dedicate the time and effort needed to become competent.

Do It Right

How many times have we heard this statement? It's a simple tenet, yet often its wisdom is ignored.

More boards and their Directors get into trouble because they choose another path when presented with a choice. Usually there are several selections offered for consideration, and the board must select among them. Instead of picking the one that's "right," the board may choose the expedient direction.

Often, making the right decision is hard. This is sometimes due to the Board having to face itself and realizing a mistake has been made or that the incorrect road was taken. Boards do not generally like to admit they are wrong or that they have made a mistake. Therefore, they tend to compound a situation of this nature by adding additional layers of misdirection.

It takes courage to face up to mistakes and "do the right thing." Attempting to hide a mistake only creates more problems. Eventually . . . sooner or later . . . it will be found out. The sense of "doing it right" easily overshadows cover-up, deceit and untruthfulness.

Respect

A Director must give respect in order to receive respect.

This human relations equation is critical to working in and being successful on a Board. If you respect others, there's a good chance they will respect you. Respect means listening to others . . . really listening. When another Director has something to say, listen carefully and as completely as possible. Take notes to make sure you understand what is being said. It could make a significant difference.

Have you ever seen a Director read a newspaper or a book during a meeting? This is a clear indication that the person does not respect the other people in the room or even the organization.

How about the people who carry on side conversations while others are talking? Not only is this disrespectful but also rude. If you are in a meeting and you see this happen, speak out and ask the chair to allow only one conversation at a time.

By respecting others' time and views, you open yourself up to receiving respect from your peers. They will also recognize that you are respectful and they can count on you to value their opinions. This is important since it helps you build positive and productive relationships.

UNITY

Confidence in the organization is strengthened by a sense of unity. It can just as easily be eroded and undermined when dissidents attack or unnecessarily question the Board.

The Board acts as a unit. As such, when a decision is made or action taken, all of the Directors are obligated to support the decision or action. No matter what the vote tally may have been, the Directors must show the members of the organization and the outside world that they agree with the outcome. They should always demonstrate that they will work together.

At meetings, Directors need to be encouraged as well as permitted to state their opinions and seek support from other Directors. They should be freely allowed, without recrimination, to take a stand on the issues or their beliefs. However, they also have to be fully aware that should their view not prevail, they must support the decision of the majority.

WILLINGNESS

A Director must be willing to serve. A person whose arm needs to be twisted is certainly not willing to be a Director. The coerced person enters the position with reticence and hesitancy. It is the start of something less than a healthy relationship and one that can, and very likely will, cause damage to the organization.

Unwilling people generally do not make good Directors. They miss meetings; they don't prepare well. They only value the position or office for the recognition it can bring them.

Oftentimes, the persuaded person is a friend or ally of a current Director whose motivation is to "pack" the Board with sympathetic people so as to achieve his or her own personal agenda.

Willingness to serve is often demonstrated when the members of an organization are surveyed and asked to serve by submitting a form or notice that confirms their feelings and intentions to work for and serve that organization.

OPEN MINDED

All too often a Director becomes blinded by his or her own issue or belief system so much so that they are unable to let another person be heard who may have a counter-point or differing view. This "closed mind" environment stifles ideas and suppresses innovation. "This is the way we've always done it" is another example of a closed mind.

Directors need to be "open minded." Meaningful and opposing conversations should be encouraged. Sharing new ideas or presenting a different approach may solve a problem the organization has faced for many years.

At the meeting, there can be a place on the agenda for "New Ideas" or "Talks for the Good of the Organization." During such discussions, Directors can talk about their dreams or concepts to change the organization or how to effectively alter its course.

LEADERSHIP

From time to time, Directors may have to make difficult decisions. It must be remembered that Directors represent their constituents and should be acting with those constituents' best interests in mind.

An issue may arise that demands sound leadership. The Director needs to carefully study the issue, consider possible outcomes and make a tough decision. Strong leadership is required to take the organization through difficult times.

The Director may face criticism or even censure for standing up for what he or she believes is right. They may be in a minority, but they still are entitled to debate and present their views. They can use facts and evidence to persuade or convince others that their position is valid and worthwhile.

DELEGATION

The Board of Directors is empowered to ensure that the organization operates smoothly and effectively. The Board does not "run" the organization.

The work and policy execution is typically delegated to staff, committees, volunteers, consultants, advisors and other persons who assist the Board in achieving the organization's goals and objectives.

The Board does not do the work! This is an important distinction. Rather, the Board makes policy and strategic decisions. The Board follows up, monitors and evaluates the implementation of those policies and decisions. This is called "macro-management."

The Board needs to know what is going on in the organization and what is being accomplished. This can be done through regular reporting. Staff, committees and others should report to the Board on a predetermined frequency. It is the staff's responsibility to ensure that the reports are completed on time and in a manner consistent with Board policy.

Too often a Board becomes entangled in the day-to-day operations of the organization. This is called "micro-managing" and can have negative and sometimes damaging effects on the staff and other work bodies.

Some Board members believe they can do a better job, so they often usurp the responsibilities of the staff. The staff is then placed in a difficult position. They will be held accountable for the results of the intruding Director, but they won't have much say about it.

Boards can solve the problem of interference by establishing performance guidelines for themselves as well as the Chief Executive Officer or perhaps the Chief Operating Officer. The CEO (or COO) establishes the guidelines for other staff members.

Performance should be evaluated on a regular basis and might even be included as a part of the regular reports.

CONFLICTS OF INTEREST

Conflicts of interest often arise when a Director has a relationship, personal interest or situation that may appear to influence, or actually does influence the judgment, decision-making or action of that Director. The relationship may be personal, professional or business related. It may be real or just "perceived."

Boards and Directors must take extra steps to avoid actual conflicts of interest and even the mere appearance of such a conflict.

An example of a conflict of interest could be a Director serving on one organization's Board and then being elected to a competing organization. Another example might be a Director who is an employee of a company either doing business with or hoping to do business with the organization.

There are many situations that may arise that can be the cause of a conflict: people change jobs, move to other areas, get married or divorced, work for different causes and have wide circles of friends and family who may influence their decisions. They need to understand that when change occurs, it may affect their standing on the Board of Directors of the organization. It is the Board's responsibility to educate its members about dealing with conflicts of interest in a positive way.

Whether the conflict is real or just perceived, it is the responsibility of the Director to disclose it to the Board of Directors. Furthermore, the Director has to inform the Board of how the conflict will be resolved. The Director should explain how his or her participation in or discussion on the issue might be a conflict of interest and, therefore, the Director should be exempted or excused from any further discussions on that particular issue.

The Board must decide the level of impact the conflict might or will have on the organization. They may recuse the Director in specific discussions or votes. The Director may be asked to leave the meeting room under certain circumstances. In some cases, if the conflict of interest is deemed to be serious enough to influence the decision-making ability of the Director, the Director may be asked to resign from the Board.

In any event, the Board needs to be both careful and thorough when dealing with conflicts of interest. The Board must also be sensitive to those conflicts and their consequences.

DIVERSITY

The Board of Directors represents the members of the organization. As such, by its very nature, the Board has to be as diverse as the breadth of those members.

Simply stated, the Board has the responsibility to do all it can to ensure the participation and involvement of all segments of the population, both professionally and culturally.

In some cases, the composition of the Board is spelled out in the Bylaws, which specifically state how the membership is to be represented.

If the Bylaws are "silent" on how to achieve diversity, the Board has to do whatever it can to open its doors and involve as many different people as possible from a variety of professional backgrounds.

In trade organizations, for example, this can translate into having various types of businesses being represented.

For public organizations, efforts would be made to involve people of different sexes, cultures, races, heritages and religions.

Failure to have diversity means that some groups are over-represented, while others may be under-represented.

CARE OF THE ORGANIZATION'S PROPERTY

As a fiduciary of an organization, it is incumbent upon a Director to protect and care for any and all of the organization's property. Property is defined not only as the hard assets, including buildings, real estate and equipment, but also includes copyrights, trademarks, goodwill and reputation. Also included is the tax-exempt status of non-profit organizations.

In particular, a Director could face liability when an organization's assets or property are sold below market value. Negligence in determining the true value of the property or willful wrongdoing can open up liability exposure for a Director involved in the transaction.

HONESTY

Honesty is not up for grabs.
A Director must be honest, period.

There is just no room for lies, cheating, stealing or dishonesty on a Board of Directors.

If you discover another Director is dishonest, it is up to you to make the challenge. Tough to do? You bet, and it takes courage and character.

However, if you allow the lying or dishonesty to continue, then you are not performing your duties properly and you deserve whatever is meted out.

If you look at the recent problems with Enron, Tyco, WorldCom and the United Way (there are many other cases), not all these Directors deserved to be painted with the same brush and color. However, they all were, and deservedly so. Because all the Directors were aware of the situation and chose to be silent, in the end, they were all just as culpable as the ones doing the mischief.

If you see a wrong, it is your obligation to do something about it. And you must do it today . . . not tomorrow or next month.

If you are unwilling to accept this responsibility, then you really should consider either not getting on the Board or resigning if you are on a Board. It's that important!

MEETINGS

Most of what happens with a Board occurs in meetings.

Meetings are those face-to-face and people-to-people occasions for communication and interchange. It's where the action is!

Organized, structured, open and smooth-flowing meetings should be the standard sought by every Board of Directors.

The Board of Directors meets frequently and regularly as directed by the Bylaws and laws of the state. The Bylaws may also specify requirements for meeting more frequently or for calling special meetings. Directors are encouraged to learn exactly what is expected of them in terms of meetings.

A Director should be fully aware of the total time commitment for meetings. When looking at the time involved, consideration must be given to preparation, travel and follow-up in addition to the actual meeting time.

Deadlines and date confirmations need to be understood and respected.

Bringing a number of people together for a meeting involves the time of many people. Treated lightly, it can be a waste of time. Directors need to be as considerate of other people's time as they expect others to be considerate of their time.

Directors need to prepare properly for a Board meeting. The agenda should be read and reviewed. If there are items to be added and changed, the Director is obligated to contact the staff and make revisions as appropriate and authorized.

Minutes, financial statements, committee reports and policy statements need to be read and reviewed prior the meeting as well. If the Director has a question or comment about an item, it can be duly noted. The staff may be able to clarify or expand an item prior to the meeting.

Directors who fail to prepare for a meeting are often embarrassed when they ask a truly "stupid" question that was answered in the materials sent out in advance. Moreover, the unprepared Director can be easily seen at the meeting turning pages and reading the material while others discuss the matter.

Meeting Attendance

The Board depends upon its Directors to participate and attend all meetings. <u>Directors are required to attend meetings, period.</u>

By missing a meeting, the Board could face a quorum shortfall.

By missing a meeting, the Director may have missed an important vote.

By missing a meeting, the Director may be perceived as not caring about the Board as much as the other Directors.

By missing a meeting, the Director is unaware of what has transpired and misses the opportunity to personally contribute. Yes, there are Minutes; however, the Minutes do not compensate for personal involvement.

It is understood that people get sick, have personal problems, encounter business conflicts and a myriad of other concerns and conditions may arise. This will happen; there is no way to ensure 100 percent attendance of all Directors, 100 percent of the time.

Directors should make it a priority in their lives that if they are going to commit to being Directors, then they will attend and actively participate in Board meetings. If they cannot make this commitment, perhaps they should back away for good or at least until they are able to honor their commitment to the Board.

Some organizations have stipulations in place that Directors missing two or more consecutive meetings can be removed from the Board or be asked to resign. It sounds harsh, but a Board cannot function properly without all of its Directors being actively involved. This includes attending meetings.

The Board commitment form emphasizes the requirement to attend meetings, and Directors sign the forms with the knowledge that they are expected to attend meetings.

QUORUM

A quorum is defined as the number of persons legally required to be in attendance for the actions taken to be legal.

Unless otherwise specified in the Bylaws, a quorum is a majority of the members of the Board who are present at the meeting and able to transact business.

For example, if the Board were comprised of fifteen members, then eight members would have to be present at the meeting to create a quorum. If the Board has twelve members, the quorum is seven members present.

Some Boards may have a fixed number, and that number is stated in the Bylaws. For example, the twelve-member Board may have a Bylaw provision that says a quorum shall be "two-thirds of the members of the Board." In this case, that means eight members would have to be present to have a quorum instead of the seven required by a simple majority.

The requirement of a quorum is a sound working principle because having an agreed upon number of persons present, ensures that issues are fully debated and actions fairly taken.

If a quorum is not present, then business cannot be transacted and the meeting has to be rescheduled.

RULES OF ORDER

Without order, there is chaos.

There must be rules of order and it is essential that a Director understand them.

Parliamentary Procedure, *Robert's Rules of Order* and the organization's own set of rules of order are several available methods to maintain and preserve order during meetings.

Robert's Rules of Order is one of the most used and quoted. Sometimes it is even incorporated into or referenced in the Bylaws. If that is the case, then those rules must be followed or a violation of the Bylaws results.

The basic premise of the rules of order is to allow for democratic speech and action and to preserve order. Without some form of order, meetings can turn into shouting matches or be monopolized by special interests.

A Director has to obtain a copy of the applicable rules. Then, the Director must read and understand them. The rules are not all that complicated and are easy to follow.

Usually they are given in hierarchal listing. By understanding the rules of order, the Director is more likely to ensure that the rules are followed, and not misused or abused. The Director may be able to affect the outcome of an issue, or even a meeting, by knowing how the rules can be effectively applied.

An important reason for the rules of order is to permit only one issue, or piece of business, to be addressed at one time. Other issues, or motions are referred, committed or tabled.

The Ayes Have It!

Most people are familiar with the usual depiction of how voting occurs. Here's how you may know it:

The president says, "All those in favor, say 'Aye!'" The Directors respond and say "Aye!" collectively.

Then the president says, "Those opposed say 'Nay!'" The Directors opposing the motion or decision say "Nay!"

Next, the president asks for abstentions, or those not voting on the issue.

The president then declares "the motion passes" or "the motion fails" based on the number of Ayes and Nays.

This type of voting probably accounts for more than ninety-five percent of Directors' votes. There are no studies or empirical data to support this statement. It is just an observation.

VOTING

Voting is the mechanism by which most of the decisions of the Board of Directors are made.

The Bylaws are specific in defining who votes, how often and when. Most of the time, the Bylaws will indicate who is entitled to "vote" and is not entitled to "vote."

This is an important distinction since some persons are permitted to attend the Board meeting but in a "non-voting" capacity. This means they can contribute suggestions, speak on issues and participate in debate; they cannot, by definition, vote on any matters.

Sometimes such a person is designated as "ex officio" because they were perhaps a past president, committee chair or held another office within the organization. Ex officio means "by virtue of the office" and unless qualified, the person will have all rights and privileges of the office. Boards may allow the placement of a political figure such as a mayor or an affiliated organization, but they do not vote or attend meetings.

To ensure that a person in this capacity does not vote, the correct phrase to use is "ex officio, non-voting." This will clearly indicate that the person has no vote.

BALLOT

There are times when a ballot is the preferred method for voting.

The most obvious reason for a written ballot is when Directors do not want to reveal how they are voting. Perhaps it is an organization whose members are competitors and disclosing how a Director votes may reveal sensitive information to a competitor. Or, it could be an embarrassing issue.

The Director simply calls for a written ballot on the issue and may even request a "secret" ballot. Usually, the president, out of respect for the requester, grants the request. However, if it becomes necessary, a vote to have the question decided by a written ballot may be required. A simple majority is all that is necessary to decide this issue unless otherwise specified by the Bylaws.

If the vote is to be by written ballot, the president appoints at least two "tellers" to count the votes. The votes are counted and the result is reported to the Board. The Minutes reflect the actual count, and whether the motion passed or failed.

MINUTES

The official record of what takes place during the Board meeting is called the Minutes. Minutes should convey all actions that were taken and decisions that were made. Minutes should not be a word for word transcription of the meeting.

The Minutes contain the date, time and location of the meeting. A list of those persons present and Directors who are absent is also included. Titles are helpful but not necessary unless specified by policy or practice.

All actions requiring a vote of the members participating in the meeting are recorded. In some cases, all that is necessary to report is that a motion was made, seconded and carried (or failed).

The actual vote tally does not always have to be recorded. However, some persons voting in favor or in opposition to an action may ask to have their names recorded. Also, some organizations may require that vote tallies be kept.

Minutes should be brief. They carry the essence of ideas and opinions expressed and often the reasons for the actions taken but not every word.

Reports given at a meeting may be appended to the Minutes and stated as such in the Minutes. There is really no reason to repeat what someone else has already written.

Minutes require timely distribution to the participants of the meeting. When distributed in a timely manner, the participants can review the Minutes while most of the meeting activities are still fresh in their minds.

Waiting for weeks or months to distribute the Minutes just means that everyone will have difficulty trying to remember what was said and done.

Minutes are usually the staff's responsibility and, therefore, the timely distribution can be incorporated as part of the staff's performance.

Minutes must be kept indefinitely as they are part of the organization's documents. It is essential the Minutes be safeguarded.

BYLAWS

The Bylaws of an organization are the rules by which the Board of Directors and members are governed. They are the glue that holds the organization together. They are important because the Bylaws provide continuity and consistency.

Bylaws are dynamic in that they can be amended to adjust or adapt to changing times. They are static as they stay the same unless amended. Amendments should not be easily approved; it's better to have some hurdles and to involve a significant portion of the membership to gain approval.

Some Bylaws require amendments by just the Board, while many require some type of majority of the organization's members. Giving the Board the power to change the Bylaws without membership involvement can be dangerous. Imagine if the U.S. Congress could change the Constitution without going to the people. Not too many people would support this idea!

It's better to involve as many members as possible when amending the Bylaws. If the proposed amendment does not achieve the majority of votes needed for passage, then the members have spoken. The Board may be disappointed, but it must be remembered that the Board does not always have the pulse of the membership, even though it thinks it does!

Occasionally, Bylaws are ignored or just not followed by some Boards. Maybe they forgot to do something as prescribed by the Bylaws, and through time, just followed the wrong procedure or process. Depending upon the amount of time that has passed, or actions taken, many or all of the activities of the Board since the infraction, could be ruled invalid. This could be troublesome since the Board may have to reverse decisions and actions that could eventually prove embarrassing and/or costly.

There are theories that say Bylaws should be open, brief and interpretable by the Board. This means that the Board can use its discretion to make a decision or determine an action. Those Boards or organizations that feel more comfortable with "loose" interpretations may prefer these types of Bylaws.

Boards or organizations that want "strict" interpretations tend to have more detailed and restrictive Bylaws. These Bylaws specifically spell out or describe what the Board is to do under prescribed conditions or events.

What are the consequences of a Board taking an action that violates or conflicts with the Bylaws? Well, the action is not legal and can be readily voided. In fact, the Board can even be sued for taking action not in compliance with its Bylaws.

PUBLIC SCRUTINY

The Board must be able to stand up to the scrutiny of its public and the people it has an effect on.

Increasingly, people are becoming more watchful of organizations whether they are for-profit or non-profit. Because of the transgressions of a few and the greed of others, Boards are no longer held in the same high regard as in previous generations.

The Board can set a course of openness and act in a way to conduct its operations above the table. By acting as if the public is looking over its shoulder, the Board becomes proactive. It has nothing to hide and its actions are open.

Another plus for openness is attracting and retaining Directors. Today, people are shying away from serving on

Boards for many reasons. One key reason is the concern that the Board may not deal openly and honestly with its activities and the Directors may be putting themselves in a position that could result in an unfortunate posture. They may have to face a legal or ethical challenge because of their service. If on the other hand, the Directors know the Board will be subject to public scrutiny and act accordingly, they may be more apt to serve.

Tax-Exempt Organizations

There is confusion about the terms "tax exempt" and "non-profit." The terms are not the same, and as such, not interchangeable. The distinction is quite clear: state law determines non-profit status but federal law determines tax exemption. Conversely, all tax-exempt organizations are non-profit, while all non-profits are not tax-exempt.

An organization is incorporated or chartered within the state of domicile. It is subject to the laws of that state that define a non-profit organization. Depending upon the nature of the organization, it may or may not be subject to state taxes. In order for an organization to even obtain a tax exempt status from the IRS, it must first prove that it is a legal entity within the state of residence.

On the federal level, organizations may apply for exemption from income tax under section 501 (a) of the Internal Revenue Code. There are 17 different recognized organizations that may qualify for exempt status. After filing the necessary application and forms, the IRS reviews the application and documents, then makes a ruling or issues a determination letter. If tax exemption status is granted, then the organization may be exempt from federal income tax.

Too many directors believe that since an organization is "non-profit," then it follows that the organization cannot make a profit. Nothing could be further from the truth. The organization needs to make a profit in order to continue its growth, and perhaps, even its existence. The non-profit designation should not have any bearing or impact upon the way the organization conducts its business and operations.

In the accounting profession, non-profit financial statements use the terms "surplus" or "excess of revenue over expenses" instead of profit. Other terms are used in regular businesses but mean virtually the same. For instance, "Statement of Financial Position" is used in place of "Balance Sheet" in a non-profit organization.

Most other aspects of the organization will be just like a regular business: a budget, legal obligations, required filings, responsibilities and challenges. The organization has to price its offerings to ensure a steady cash flow in order to satisfy members and stakeholders. It needs to recruit and retain talented and experienced personnel, just like a for-profit business.

Non-profit organizations may or may not be exempt from federal and state taxes. If you are in a non-profit organization, consider checking with the CEO or staff accountant to ascertain the exemption. Ask for a copy of the IRS determination letter or ruling. The document will clearly explain the status of the organization.

Remember, non-profit is only a tax status designation; it is not a business model.

COMPENSATION

Depending upon the type of organization and its By-laws, Directors may receive compensation.

Generally, non-profit organizations do not compensate Directors. Most of the times, this prohibition is stated in the Bylaws. Moreover, should the organization discontinue its operations for any reason, the Bylaws usually state that no funds of the organization shall inure to any Director. This inurement is usually extended to members of the non-profit organization as well.

There are people who believe that Directors should be compensated because they contribute time, energy, talents and perhaps even money to the organization they serve.

Compensation of Directors of a non-profit organization may constitute a conflict of interest. After all, a non-profit organization is chartered for the good of the public. If Directors are able to make decisions and guide the organization for their own benefit by receiving compensation, then the mission of the organization may become clouded or even compomised.

Compensation of Directors in a for-profit organization is a different matter. Many for-profit organizations compensate their Directors. The Directors in this arena knowingly become Directors because they will be compensated. They work for the entity, bringing forth their expertise or experience, the very reason they were selected. They are paid to attend Board and committee meetings and sometimes they are asked to perform specific duties.

Directors of for-profit organizations may also work in some other capacity for the organization. They may be officers or managers. They may be shareholders. What ever their positions, there should be no conflict of interest since they are acting in the best interests of the organization.

EXCESS COMPENSATION

When Directors are compensated for their time, it is vitally important that the compensation be commensurate with the levels of compensation within the industry.

Excess compensation can be defined as a person receiving more money than the position is usually entitled to or recognized as the standard for that position. There are usually comparative compensation studies or surveys available with the Board's particular industry or field of endeavor. These studies generally outline the position descriptions, duties and responsibilities of the Directors.

Should the survey show compensation above the norm for the position, the IRS may consider the person to be "excessively compensated." In this case, either the organization or the individual may be subject to additional taxes and/or penalties.

The same is true for the organization's staff and especially the chief executive officer of the organization. If it is determined that the CEO received or is receiving excess compensation, damage to the organization can be extensive. One only has to look at the New York Stock Exchange (NYSE) to see the unbelievable excessive compensation received by its former CEO. Not only has it impugned the integrity of NYSE and its Directors, but is has also cast a huge, dark cloud over the entire industry.

REIMBURSEMENT

Directors have the right to be reimbursed for reasonable expenses they incur on behalf of the organization.

Regardless of the type of organization, non-profit or for-profit, Directors should be able to recover funds personally expended for the organization.

Reimbursed expenses typically include travel, lodging, telephone, and postage. Sometimes, these expenses are referred to as "out-of-pocket" expenses.

The Board must have a published statement explaining its expense reimbursement policy. The policy needs to be specific and outline just what expenses are considered reimbursable. For example, air travel may be limited to coach airfare with advance purchase. Another example may be the rate of mileage reimbursement. Some organizations merely mirror the rate as set by the IRS each year; others establish their own rate.

Directors should sign the statement acknowledging that they have read and understand the policy.

The policy should also provide instructions on how and when reimbursements are to be made. Actual receipts should be required for all reimbursed expenses; copies of vouchers, bills and statements should be avoided.

In some cases, and depending upon the size of the organization, an approval should be obtained from some other person not on the Board. This could be an assistant treasurer, staff accountant or controller.

It is helpful to have a standard organizational form that has the columns, spaces and entries for easy completion. Forms are available at most office supply stores as well as numerous Internet sources.

INDEMNIFICATION

Some organizations indemnify their Directors against any and all financial liability for serving on the Board of Directors. Included in this indemnification can be actual settlement amounts. The indemnification is generally incorporated in the Bylaws.

Indemnification is granted, however, only if the Director acted in good faith and in the best interests of the organization. If the Director acted in bad faith, or was otherwise liable, then the defense legal fees and any settled amounts may be borne by the Director and not the organization.

Some states may allow indemnification and others may require it, especially for non-profit organizations. A Director should check the state in question as laws may vary state-to-state. Indemnification is mandated by some states should the Director successfully defend a legal claim.

The expense of the indemnification is usually funded by the organization and not the individual Director. Some insurance carriers offer coverage for indemnification, and Directors are encourage to investigate this avenue to make certain they are covered.

In addition, a Director should have a written outline of what is covered and the extent to which he or she is covered.

Of course, the indemnification is good only to the extent that the organization has the wherewithal to pay legal fees and other expenses should a claim be filed.

DIRECTORS AND OFFICERS INSURANCE

A Director should require the organization to have Directors and Officers Insurance coverage. Often called "D & O" insurance, it usually covers the officers and the Board from suits brought against them for legal activities. The caution here is that D & O Insurance will not cover illegal actions or acts, and officers will be responsible for their own defense.

Coverages should be reviewed and explained to Directors since policies and companies vary in their definitions, coverages and exclusions. Not being aware of what the coverage entails, and how deep it is, can be costly to a Director when a lawsuit is filed.

Most lawsuits and claims against Boards and organizations are employee-based. Wrongful termination and sexual harassment cases are examples. Coverage is also needed for antitrust activities, copyright/trademark infringement, defamation and breach of fiduciary duties.

D & O Insurance is generally paid for by the organization.

Antitrust Considerations

The federal government, or people who believe they have been harmed, can sue Boards of Directors and any other individuals who act on behalf of the organization and who violate the antitrust laws.

It is very important that organizations, and particularly non-profit organizations, have "antitrust guidelines" that specifically outline and detail what activities and behaviors are not permitted. These guidelines prohibit:

1. Restraint of trade, regardless of what the code of conduct or ethics calls for;
2. Exclusion or expulsion of membership for competitors;
3. Standards or certification programs that harm competitors; and,
4. Price-fixing discussions.

The courts have held Directors and others from organizations, including volunteers in non-profit groups, can be personally liable for antitrust violations. Some have paid huge fines; others have served time in jail.

Antitrust issues are a serious matter, and Directors must be aware of the consequences. Even if there is no direct antitrust involvement by the individual, the Director can be charged with mismanagement or negligence by allowing the conduct to occur or continue.

Directors must be alert as to what constitutes antitrust behavior, recognize it and then take appropriate action to discontinue such activities without delay.

VOLUNTEER PROTECTION

Directors serving on non-profit Boards may have liability protection either by the federal government or states.

Volunteer protection statutes have been adopted by the federal government and most states (where many non-profit organizations are incorporated) in order to provide liability protection and relief for Directors. The depth and coverage vary greatly in the state laws, but the federal statute provides broad protection. Some states merely have the burden of proof raised for plaintiff's actions. Others offer protection only for the organization, while some have protection for only the Directors.

To understand exactly what the protection may be, Directors may need to review the Volunteer Protection statutes in:

1. The state in which they reside;
2. The state in which the organization is incorporated;

3. The state in which the organization currently resides or has its main office; and

4. The U. S. government statutes.

If a suit or claim is brought against a Director, there probably will be discussions regarding where the case will be handled since it may be difficult to determine what location takes preference.

SARBANES-OXLEY ACT

The Sarbanes-Oxley Act (SOX) of 2002 outlines federal criminal penalties and auditing requirements. It was enacted after a public furor arose because of the mishandling and mismanagement of several publicly traded corporations. Directors and officers of those organizations claimed they did not know the financial condition of the organization. Now, SOX makes them accountable.

It is important to note that under SOX, Directors of publicly traded companies are responsible to make certain the organization complies with the law. Basically, SOX calls for proper maintenance and retention of documents and records pertaining to the specifics of auditing the organization's finances.

One provision of SOX applies equally to non-profit organizations as well as publicly traded corporations. Documents cannot be altered, destroyed, concealed or mutilated to the extent that their use, integrity or availability is impeded or impaired in an official proceeding.

SOX also covers intent and any attempts to change files or documents.

Fines or imprisonment may face violators of SOX. Also penalties may be imposed on persons who obstruct, influence or impede any official proceeding or attempt to do so.

There is a "Whistle Blower" protection provision built into SOX that also applies to non-profit organizations. This provision prohibits retaliation or any other harmful action against any person providing truthful information to law enforcement officials relating to the commission, or possible commission, of a federal offense.

SOX requires auditor independence for audits. Under the new guidelines, auditors should not audit their own work. Auditors also should not provide "non-audit services," such as consulting, when these services become involved in the decision making of management or in the performance of management functions. Auditors should not provide non-audit services if those services are significant or material to the auditor's subject matter. Under the new standards, there are exceptions to these rules but certain safeguards must exist or be implemented.

Under SOX, corporate CEOs and CFOs must personally certify their familiarity with the financial reports, legal compliance, material accuracy and disclosures to both the public and the audit committee. Additionally, loans to Directors and officers are prohibited.

Although most provisions of SOX do not apply to non-profit organizations, the themes of accountability, transparency and responsibility should guide Directors' behavior.

AUDIT COMMITTEE

Under the Sarbanes-Oxley Act, publicly held companies are required to form audit committees. These committees are to be comprised of independent Directors.

The responsibility of the audit committee is to review all financial reports and supervise and oversee external audits.

It is a very important task. The people on this committee must be carefully selected. They should not have any conflicts of interest or even the appearance of any conflicts of interest.

Privately held and non-profit organizations should consider setting up audit committees if none exist. It's only a matter of time before this area of oversight will impact other arenas.

FORBIDDEN FRUIT

There is a saying in the business world, "Don't dip your pen in the company ink."

The meaning is simple: as a Director, don't mess around with other Board members, staff, contractors, attorneys or others working with or for the Board. This is another one of those rules that simply must be observed and practiced.

The temptation may be great for a Director to engage a staff member, for example, and begin a journey that may be hurtful not only to the Director and staff member but also to the entire Board. It can be the beginning of a conflict of interest that will derail plans and destroy dreams.

Sexual harassment is an area that must be avoided at all costs and Directors must be informed and educated to avoid any appearance of harassment of any kind. Remember, a Director sets the example. He or she is the leader and may be liable under the law for inappropriate advances to staff members.

The Director does not use his or her power or authority to enter into a romantic relationship.

Human emotions are difficult to control, however. So, it is possible for two people to meet and begin a relationship. Boards cannot control feelings, but Boards can control where those feelings are shown or displayed.

If you are a Director and fall madly in love with a staff member, or the organization's lawyer, or even another Director on the same Board, you really must resign immediately. Take this action before the relationship becomes a problem.

LAWYERS

The Board of Directors needs to have legal guidance and advice. In today's world, it is no longer a matter of choice; it is a necessity.

Legal counsel should attend all Board meetings, review and approve the agenda, review and approve the Minutes of the meeting and offer advice as needed or appropriate.

It must be remembered that legal counsel is retained or employed to represent the organization but works with the Board. If the legal counsel is unsure of whom they represent, get another lawyer!

This is an important point. The lawyer may have to make a decision or render an opinion that is unpopular with the Board and needs to understand that the members of the organization may be negatively impacted by a Board action or decision. The lawyer needs courage and wisdom to counter the Board's zeal or enthusiasm.

Some lawyers will offer counsel to a Board and then

also do business with members. This may be a conflict of interest and should be avoided. Lawyers must be very careful if they work for members while also serving the Board.

A good way to avoid conflicts and make certain the lawyer understands who the client is, is to have a simple agreement prepared that clarifies the role of legal counsel.

Executive Sessions

Some Boards believe that executive sessions are a means to facilitate discussions without risk or liability. Generally, these sessions are "closed" to staff and involve a discussion of executive or confidential topics that a Director or Directors believe should be private.

Executive sessions can lead to trouble! There are several reasons to discourage the practice.

Most executive sessions have no agenda. Discussions can wander and may enter areas in which Directors should not be involved.

Seldom are Minutes kept, even though they should be. If troubles arise for the organization, the participants of the closed-door meeting have no proof as to what was said or what actions were taken. All organization meetings deserve good Minutes.

Executive sessions have the potential to damage the relationship between the Board and the staff. Excluding staff from a meeting creates the natural assumption that there is some reason . . . real or perceived . . . that they should not be included. A possible negative result is a criticism or judgment of performance.

Suspicion or misunderstandings can also result since the staff has no opportunity to respond. Further, the staff can be a sounding board and provide accurate responses that are factual.

Executive sessions can easily turn into complaint sessions. The Board chair that lets Directors put anything on the table is truly opening Pandora's Box. Instead of solving problems or addressing issues, the Board may just be creating new difficulties.

Closed-door sessions encourage rumors. People are quick to gossip about what goes on behind those doors. Inaccurate information may be passed on as fact simply because a person in a leadership position mentioned it.

A Director may arrange for an executive session as a way to promote his or her personal agenda behind closed doors. We all know people who use an organization to further their own selfish interests. Open meetings insure that a personal agenda takes a backseat to the organization's business.

EXECUTIVE COMMITTEES

Executive Committees serve an important role, but some times they can also be harmful to the health of the organization!

The generally recognized purpose of the Executive Committee is to make decisions or take action during the time lapse between Board meetings or to fulfill other "specific" duties assigned by the Board. That's all it should be . . . if at all!

Remember, the Board as a whole is responsible for the organization. It may delegate its authority in some cases to committees or persons for certain activities; however, the Board still retains overall responsibility. The Board cannot abdicate this obligation.

Some Boards "entrust" the Executive Committee with far too much power. Be careful! Keep the Executive Committee in your sites and do not allow it to exceed its authority.

If the organization has an Executive Committee, be

certain that its purpose and limits are clearly defined. The Executive Committee must keep Minutes of all of its meetings, including conference calls. These Minutes then have to be reviewed and approved by the Board at its next meeting.

In today's world, with improved technology and communication, the need for an Executive Committee is greatly reduced. For issues requiring action by the Board, but apart from a meeting, electronic voting often can be utilized. With email and faxes ... and conference calls ... the entire Board can be brought together just as easily as the Executive Committee.

Please check with your counsel or state about the laws governing your organization's voting.

THE ABILENE PARADOX

Directors should guard against trips to Abilene!
Jerry Harvey discussed this always-timely subject in his management book, *The Abilene Paradox*. In the book, a group of people traveled some distance in a non-air conditioned car, to a restaurant none of them liked individually, for food they did not want, and when each had something else better to do.

"Group dynamics, group decisions," Harvey says.

A group of people such as a Board of Directors can become so caught up that they lose sight of where they are going, and for that matter, why they are going there.

Many Boards "take trips to Abilene." Decisions are made by the group that individuals would never make alone. However, the individuals go along because they either don't want to be left out or to be seen as laggards. They want to be seen as "regulars," not as dissenters.

The group becomes all-powerful and to be a dissenter, even though you may be right in doing so, can result in negative behavior on the part of the Board. The dissenter can be ridiculed, disparaged, humiliated or even ostracized. No one wants that.

Directors who do not want to take a "trip to Abilene" should make sure they are in an environment where they can speak freely and openly. The Boardroom should be a place where opposing views are expressed. No one should be excoriated for expressing a personal position or feeling.

If you are on a Board that is taking a trip, or planning a trip to Abilene, then please buy each Director a copy of Mr. Harvey's book and discuss it at the next meeting. It will be worth the cost!

ORIENTATION

Directors are entitled to an orientation to the Board. Whether formal or informal, a new Director should be given the opportunity to learn about the Board, i.e., strategic plan, objectives, policies, procedures, tradition, fiduciary duties and more. This is as simple as using a binder.

The organization should have the binder appropriately tabbed with key areas. Each area should contain up-to-date information such as the latest Minutes, financial statements and committee reports. The binder is a resource tool and should be kept by the Director for his or her term of office. When the term is completed, the binder should be returned.

Some organizations place this information in a password-protected, secure area of their Web site. Directors can then have 24/7 access. This is an excellent method of maintaining up-to-date information. However, it is up to the individuals to access the file and review it on their own. The risk is that the information may not be studied or reviewed in a complete manner.

The preferred method is always face-to-face, formal meeting with new Directors. A "run-through" of the information occurs and is followed by questions and answers. The new Director receives immediate responses to questions and probably will have a better understanding of the processes and operations of the organization.

STRATEGIC PLANNING

To succeed, an organization needs to have a vision and a plan. The strategic plan becomes the "roadmap" for the future. It serves as a guide for the Board, committees and staff. It combines all the ingredients of the organization into one coordinated effort that helps the organization grow in an organized and orderly fashion.

With a strategic plan, the Board has a clearer direction for advancing the goals of the organization over a longer period of time. This major benefit of the strategic plan encourages "forward thinking" by the Board.

Plans generally cover a period of three to five years, although recent trends have been shorter periods of one to three years. The time period is not as important as the construction of the plan itself.

The plan also can help to identify target markets and reveal opportunities while recognizing barriers and detecting weaknesses. There is no set formula for this activity, as each organization is unique and impacting factors vary from organization to organization.

There are seven generally recognized elements of a strategic plan: a mission statement, a situational analysis, goals and objectives, strategies and tactics, the written plan, implementation, and finally, controls and metrics. The situational analysis can also be referred to as "environmental scan."

Plans are not required to be lengthy or unwieldy. Some plans can be brief and outlined on a single sheet of paper. Others may require a large binder or complex computer model. The key here is that the size of the plan should fit the organization, and not the converse. It is imperative that the plan be written and published. Without this step, it would be nearly impossible to track its progress.

Communicating the plan to directors, members, stakeholders and customers is important. It demonstrates the commitment the Board has to advance its mission and the goals of the organization.

ENDING

"The Perfect Board" is probably a goal that can never be reached. Given the manner in which people work with one another, it is doubtful that consistent harmony can be achieved.

But maybe that is the goal! Working together . . . moving the organization forward, instead of individual or selfish pursuits.

People can help guide by using the principles and tenets of *The Perfect Board*. It is not always easy to take a position and stand up for a principle, but if more people did, the organization and our country would be so much better off.

Sharing and discussing ideas is a meaningful experience. Most often Boards are consumed with the business of the day and rarely explore the underlying principles and ideals of character. Placing a topic such as integrity or leadership or competency on the agenda could offer a truly rewarding experience. Imagine how the Directors might offer their definitions on the selected subject. See how some may wriggle while dealing with a sensitive topic. See how they present themselves and learn their positions.

Some will say that it is a waste of time to discuss lofty principles or ideas because time is so precious. They will say, "Let's get on with business and if there is any time remaining in the meeting, then we can talk about extraneous stuff."

The "extraneous stuff" may be the actual business and how it is handled. Far better are the agreed-upon ideals coming into practice because people understand them and are not afraid of insisting on them.

Some wish we could return to past years when virtue and character were more highly regarded. There was more civility. People seemed to care. Part of this was due to the fact that many were educated with expectations of character and civility. They learned it. Today, many people don't understand the importance of these traits because they have not learned them.

The responsibility for learning how to treat others falls upon the Board as well as the individual Director. They must teach each other as well as showing the way for the new arrivals.

Through cooperation, learning, teaching and practicing, Directors can truly be on their way to a more "Perfect Board."

Dinner With E.J.

Becca finished reading the book, closed it and then sat back in the chair. She thought for a moment, *What a great introduction to what I'll be doing.*

She arose from the chair and placed the book on E.J.'s desk. She walked to the door and left the room heading down the hall to the kitchen area.

"Oh, hello, Olivia," she said as she greeted E.J.'s helper.

"Hello, Rebecca. You want something to drink?"

"Yes, please. Do you have anymore of the lemonade I had earlier?"

"Oh, yes. I'll get you some with fresh ice."

Becca asked, "Where is Mr. E.J.?"

"He went into town for a short trip. He said he needed something special."

Olivia handed the cold glass of lemonade to Becca.

"Thank you, Olivia." She took a sip. "This is very refreshing."

"You're welcome. I make it every day for Mr. E.J. He likes it very much."

"Do you have an idea when he will return?"

"Gibsonville is not far. It's about twenty minutes each way. He left shortly after he closed the door to his office. He told me not to disturb you, but if you asked for anything, I should get it for you. He said he would not be gone too long."

"Well, Olivia, I guess I'll just sit on one of those rocking chairs and finish my lemonade."

"Yes, that would be nice. Oh, oh, Mr. E.J. was wondering if you would be staying for dinner. Are you?"

"I hadn't planned on it."

"Oh, Rebecca, he does not ask many people to dinner. You should feel proud that he is thinking of you. You must be special."

"Special? I don't think so. But then it's not up to me to know what's in his heart. Dinner, *hmmn*?"

"It is a long drive home, is it not, Rebecca?"

"Yes, it is a long journey, and I am feeling hungry all of a sudden."

"It's my lemonade. It perks up the appetite. Mr. E.J. says that every day. Here, you go sit on the porch and I'll bring some snacks to tide you over until we eat."

"Did I say I was staying for dinner?"

"Maybe not say, but your eyes sure said yes."

Becca sat in the rocking chair. It was late afternoon and it was quite warm. The breeze off the river was cool. With the shade of the porch and the moving air, it was a very comfortable place to be.

Olivia brought cheese, crackers and some cut up vegetables. Becca munched the snacks and sipped the lemonade. It was very pleasant just to sit.

"Hello there!" a voice barked around the corner. "You must be a fast reader. I did not think you'd be finished by now."

She recognized E.J. as he stepped onto the porch. He was carrying a large brown bag.

"Maybe I am a fast reader, but I think it had more to do with the subject matter. It was so interesting. I could not put it down. You're an excellent writer."

"Thanks for the compliment. Did Olivia ask you to stay for dinner?"

"Yes, she did."

"Well, don't keep me in suspense. Are you staying?"

"I am kind of hungry even with these treats she brought to me."

"She's the best, isn't she?" Becca nodded.

"Then you're staying?" Becca nodded again.

"Great! I went into town and got some fresh sea bass. I hope you like fish."

"Love it."

"That's wonderful because Olivia prepares sea bass Vera Cruz. She broils the fish and tops it with fresh salsa, olives and capers. It is so delicious and one of my favorites. What do you think?

"Sounds wonderful," Becca replied.

"Let me take this bag of groceries to her. We'll eat in about an hour if that's alright with you."

"It's okay by me. I really appreciate the invitation to dinner."

"My pleasure. I don't get very many guests, or I should I say people that I like!!

"That's kind of you to say, E.J."

He went inside and delivered the bag. She could hear him walking to the office. She heard him walk down the hallway and as he neared the door, he opened it and stepped out onto the porch. He was holding the large green book.

"Well, young lady, what did you think of *The Perfect Board?*"

He sat in the adjacent rocking chair leaning back with the book on his lap. He looked at her.

"E.J., I think the book is excellent. You should publish it. It is so simple, yet it covers so much information a Board member can use. It really will help me do my job."

"I am glad you liked it."

"Like it? I marvel at it. All that knowledge in one little book."

"Well, that's what I meant for it to do. I want people to believe in themselves when they are invited to sit on a board. I want to make sure they understand what is expected of them and the Boards they serve."

"I believe they will," exclaimed Becca.

EPILOGUE

Rebecca Mayfield was elected to the Board of Directors.

Because she was prepared and aware of the responsibilities and duties of a Director, she accepted the position.

At her first meeting, Becca shared with the other Board members her desire to be an active Board member. She indicated that she was sensitive to current policies, but independent in her thinking and actions. She asked about the Policy Manual and requested a copy for review. And, she took the time to read and study it thoroughly.

As a result, in subsequent meetings, Becca was able to establish new policies on Sexual Harassment and Antitrust Avoidance. She also was the initiator of the Board of Directors' Code of Conduct and developed the organization's first confirmation forms. She worked well and cooperatively with the other Board members.

Her most important contribution was very likely the development of the Executive Sessions Policy, ensuring that these meetings would be made more open, identify items to be discussed in advance and require that the actions taken would be officially recorded so that they could be ratified at the next Board of Directors meeting. Members had expressed their concern that Executive Sessions had become "too secretive" because they were being convened without published agendas, did not have minutes nor did they involve staff.

At first, the other Directors scoffed at Becca's interest and enthusiasm. They asked her why she didn't just go along with what other members of the Board wanted as new Board members had always done in the past?

Becca responded by saying she took the job of being a Director seriously. She once told the Board, "I have no hidden agenda. I am not trying to run this organization. I simply want the organization to function well."

About a year later, Becca telephoned E.J. When she heard his voice and pleasant greetings, she said, "E.J., I want to thank you for the guidance you provided to me. Your book helped me step into the Board as if I really had the experience and knowledge to be on a Board. Without that support and prior knowledge, I am not sure what I would have done."

E.J. remarked, "Becca, I am glad everything is working out. I might add that the challenge is never over. It is always there. People change. Issues change. The Director has to always be vigilant and keep his or her perspective, as long as he or she serves."

She replied, "Yes, I know that now.

E.J. continued, "You will do well as a Director, because you truly care about the organization that you are trying to serve, what it means and the value it brings to both its members and the public. I feel it in my heart that you will be moving on to more and greater challenges of leadership in the future. You are perfect for the Board."

Becca closed the call. "I appreciate your confidence in me E.J. It means a lot to me."

She paused. "E.J. Hmmn. The Perfect Board?"

"Yes, Becca," he repeated.

"Well, it means a lot to me also! If it hadn't been for you, I am not sure where I would have wandered. I hope other people will see The Perfect Board and have their lives changed too."

BIBLIOGRAPHY

Carver, John. *Boards That Make a Difference*, San Francisco: Jossey-Bass, 1997.

Clemons, Calvin, and Robert Harris. *Building an Association Management Company*, Tallahassee, FL, 1997.

Collins, Jim. *Good to Great*, New York: Harper/Collins Publishing, 2001.

Dunlop, James. *Leading the Association*, Washington, D.C.: American Society of Association Executives, 1989.

Eadie, Douglas. *Boards That Work*, Washington, D.C.: American Society of Association Executives, 1989.

Ernstthal, Henry, CAE. *Principles of Association Management*, 4th ed., Washington, D.C.: American Society of Association Executives, 1989.

Harris, Robert. *Board Excellence Workbook*, Tallahassee, FL: Nonprofit Center, 2004.

Harris, Robert. *How to Create a Policy Manual*, Tallahassee, FL: Nonprofit Center, 2004.

Harris, Robert. *How to Be an Association Executive/Chamber CEO*, Tallahassee, FL: Nonprofit Center, 2004.

Harvey, Jerry. *The Abilene Paradox and Other Meditations on Management*, San Francisco: Jossey-Bass, 1996.
Howe, Fisher. *Welcome to the Board*, San Francisco: Jossey-Bass, 1995.

Jacobs, Jerald. *Association Law Handbook*, 3rd ed., Washington, D.C.: Bureau of National Affairs, 1996.

Sherman, John. *The New Robert's Rules of Order*, Barnes & Noble, 1993.

Robert's Rules of Order, 2nd ed., Indianapolis: Wiley Publishing, 2001.

Zadel, Greg. *Your Director Hat*, Firestone, CO, 2003.